Animal & Birds

Fish

Fish are water animals with fins and scales that help them to swim.

Quick Fact
Did you know that fish cannot stay in the Dead Sea as there is too much salt in it.

Amphibians

Amphibians are animals that spend a part of their lives under water and the remaining part on land.

Quick Fact
Amphibians breathe through their skin. Their skin takes in oxygen and water.

Reptiles

Reptiles are animals which are cold blooded and have scales on their bodies. They lay eggs.

Quick Fact
Snakes and lizards flick their tongues in the air to capture the scent of particles. They don't smell through their noses. They use their tongues to collect scent of particles!

Birds

Birds are animals which can fly and have feather on their bodies. Birds too lay eggs like reptiles.

Quick Fact
Ostrich is the largest bird in the whole bird kingdom.

Mammals

Mammals are animals which have hair on their bodies. The mother feeds her young ones with her milk.

Quick Fact
The hippopotamus gives birth under water and nurses its young there. But the young hippos do come up periodically for air.

Marsupials

Marsupials are a group of animals whose females carry and feed their young in their pouches.

Quick Fact
A male kangaroo is called a boomer, a female kangaroo a flyer, and a baby kangaroo a joey.

Primates

Primates are a kind of mammals which have proper hands and feet with five fingers each. These include humans, great apes, monkeys and lemurs.

Quick Fact
Did you know that monkeys never catch cold!

What is life cycle?

Life cycle of mammals

Life cycle is the process of growing up from childhood to adulthood.

- Birth
- Feeding
- Young dogs or puppies
- Adulthood

Life cycle of a frog

- Egg mass
- Tadpole
- Tadpole with legs
- Young frog
- Adult frog

Life cycle of insects

Life cycle of a butterfly

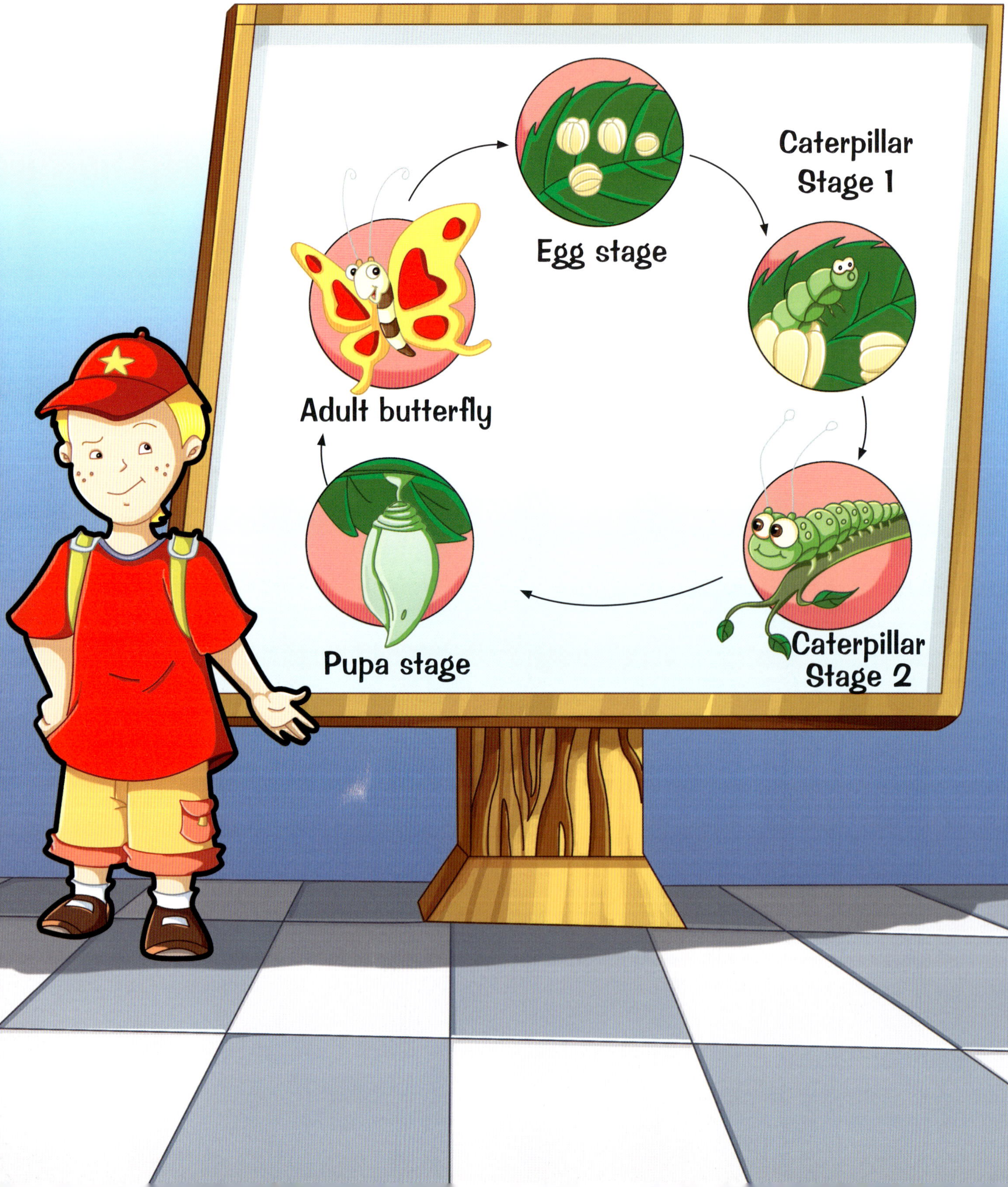

- Egg stage
- Caterpillar Stage 1
- Caterpillar Stage 2
- Pupa stage
- Adult butterfly

Life cycle of a crocodile

- Laying eggs
- Hatching
- Youthful stage
- Becoming an adult
- Adult stage

Adaptation

Structural adaptation

Animals often use their teeth, scales, fur, bottlenose and feathers to survive in the environment they live in.

- Fur
- Teeth
- Scales
- Feathers
- Bottlenose

Migration

When animals and birds move from one place to another and then back again to their original place it is called migration. They do this to find better climate, better food and a safe place to live in.

Quick Fact
Most birds fly at night in small flocks. This allows them to eat during the day and saves them from enemies.

Colouration

Many a time animals and even insects change colour to protect themselves from enemies. This is called colouration.

Quick Fact
Tuatara is one of the most remarkable animals which can change colour to protect itself.